Pocket Charts
for Math

Easy How-tos & Reproducible Templates
for Making 15 Interactive Pocket Charts
That Teach Primary Math Skills

by Valerie SchifferDanoff

SCHOLASTIC
PROFESSIONAL BOOKS

NEW YORK • TORONTO • LONDON • AUCKLAND • SYDNEY
MEXICO CITY • NEW DELHI • HONG KONG

Dedicated to my son Zachary Mattey in celebration
of his math sense, sensitivity, sensibility, and even his nonsense.

∽

I wish to acknowledge Kelly Swanson for her help and her color sense.

∽

Cover design by Jaime Lucero and Norma Ortiz
Interior design by Solutions by Design, Inc.
Illustrations by Rusty Fletcher

ISBN: 0-590-98336-9

Printed in the U.S.A.

Table of Contents

Introduction

NUMBERS, NUMBERS

Numbers in the grocery store
About the things we eat.
Numbers on the doorways,
And in the city street.
Numbers on the calendar,
On signs that flash or flow.
Numbers on the telephone,
Or tickets for the show.
Numbers on the buses,
On the money that I spend.
Numbers on the stamps I put
On letters that I send.
Numbers on the highways, yes,
And numbers in a book!
It seems I'm seeing numbers
Almost anywhere I look.

— *"Numbers, Numbers" by Lee Blair from* Arithmetic in Verse and Rhyme *by
Allan D. Jacobs and Leland B. Jacobs, 1976. By permission of Allen D. Jacobs.*

As this poem illustrates, numbers are everywhere! So it's no surprise that children are primed and ready to delve into math learning from a very early age. And what better way to teach them than with the hands-on, child-friendly world of pocket charts?

As the use of pocket charts in early childhood and elementary classrooms becomes more popular, teachers are realizing that these hands-on learning tools lend themselves to an array of curriculum areas—and math is no exception! Pocket charts and math are a perfect combination *and* a great way to forge a natural connection between literacy and numeracy. A wide variety of math skills ranging from addition to shapes, simple fractions to skip counting, can be presented in a visual, hands-on, and highly engaging manner using standard pocket charts and the step-by-step how-tos in this book.

The activities presented here are easy to prepare for, and do not require expensive or difficult to find materials. For most, you'll need only sentence strips, access to a photocopier, scissors, and magic markers. And here's more good news: If the finished strips and picture templates are stored carefully, they can be used again and again to delight your students for many years to come.

Meeting the NCTM Standards With Pocket Charts

15 Pocket Charts for Math provides fun activities that introduce and reinforce essential primary concepts including number sense, geometry, measurement, and pre-multiplication. The NCTM Standards were used as a guiding principle in devising charts that will foster the use of manipulative materials, build literacy, encourage discussions and cooperative work, and enhance your students' questioning skills. Because this book correlates with the standards, it is recommended that you consider teaching the charts in the order presented. However, you should feel free to use them in any sequence you see fit—after all, you know your students best.

Tips for Hanging and Displaying Pocket Charts

Pocket charts can be used for an astonishing number of purposes anywhere in the classroom. They can be used for whole-class instruction during circle time, small-group lessons, or hands-on learning centers where kids can "play" with the text independently.

Pocket charts are easily displayed in many different ways. They can be hung on a bul-

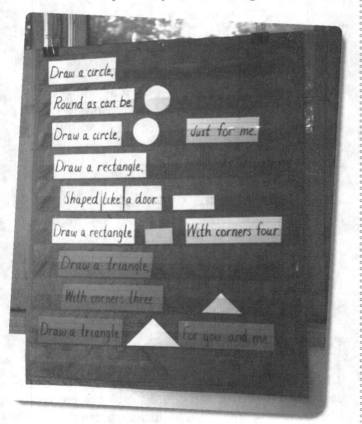

letin board and secured by heavy-duty push-pins or on an easel with easel clips. Heavy-duty Velcro can also be used to hang pocket charts on walls or from shelves. Pocket chart stands are also available at teaching supply stores and in catalogs.

You may find that pocket charts tend to curl inward when suspended. Placing a thin dowel cut to the width of the chart in the last pocket, behind the sentence strip, can alleviate the problem. Dowels *cut to size* can be purchased at hardware, home stores, and craft shops.

When hanging pocket charts for young learners, be especially aware of the height. Pocket charts are marvelously adaptable; they can be hung at just the right height for children to use. Children love to be able to walk up to a chart at eye level and easily manipulate the sentence strips. So many things are frustratingly out of a child's reach, so it's a real plus that a pocket chart can be adjusted to the perfect height.

Sizes of Pocket Charts and Sentence Strips

Pocket charts are available in a variety of sizes and colors, as are sentence strips. The typical pocket chart is 34" x 42" with ten pockets. This size offers you the most versatility as it can be used in activities with the whole class, as well as in learning centers. Another option that allows for a variety of settings is 42" high by 58" wide. This chart also has ten pockets and is almost twice the size of the average pocket chart. The width can easily be divided to display two or more different activities by hanging blank sentence strips vertically or by using a piece of colored masking tape. If you are able to purchase more than one pocket chart, a 24" x 24" chart is also available and is perfect for learning centers and other small spaces.

Pocket charts are most commonly manufactured in blue. However, the Teaching Resource Center Catalog (1-800-833-3389) has charts in red, pink, lavender, blue, yellow,

green, and white.

The best sentence strips for use in pocket charts are of tag-quality paper, precut to 3" x 24". These are available in white, beige, and packs of assorted pastel colors. If you are able to purchase several different colors of strips, you can use them in many ways. For example, the answer to an equation can be done in a different color from that of the equation. Children enjoy displays that are visually pleasing, and a variety of colors will be appreciated. Throughout this book, optional color choices are given. If you are able to buy several colors, try using the optional color choices. Please note, however, that the lessons will still work wonderfully if only one color is used.

Storing Sentence Strips

Sentence strips can be stored by theme, skill, or concept. They can be stored in a flat folder made by folding a large piece of cardboard in half. A butterfly clip, large paper clip, or small clamp can be used to keep the strips needed for individual lessons together.

While teaching staff development courses, other teachers who enjoy using pocket charts have volunteered their storage solutions, including:

☆ long-stem flower box, which most florists stock

☆ cardboard wall-paper box, cut along the top

☆ box in which the sentence strips arrived, covered with contact paper

☆ two manila folders, opened, folded length-wise and attached with tape

☆ wall-paper glue tray

Teaching Techniques for Pocket Charts

When using pocket charts in the early childhood classroom, it is important to take into consideration the development and experience of your children. A kindergarten student may never have seen a pocket chart before, so it is very helpful to demonstrate the basic steps one follows in a lesson. When you are using the pocket chart for the first time, consider doing something that is of great interest to the child, such as spelling out the names of individual children and asking the class to point to the person whose name is on the board.

Here are some other tips to keep in mind when teaching with pocket charts:

☆ Be specific when modeling how to use the components in a pocket chart lesson; what seems obvious to you may be confusing to a child.

☆ Teach children how to place words,

sentence strips, and picture templates in the pocket chart and how to carefully remove them.

☆ When brainstorming ideas during a pocket chart lesson, encourage everyone to participate.

☆ Write entire words or sentences on sentence strips and then cut them apart. These can then be arranged in the pockets.

☆ When reading from a pocket chart, encourage children to read with you. Point to each word as you read.

☆ When teaching a short poem, chant or repeat the verses or rhymes for emphasis. You will find that the class will establish a rhythm. Encourage children to repeat the poem using this rhythm. Children love to chant sets of rhyming words.

☆ Use pictures, either in addition to or instead of words. This allows children to match words to pictures and pictures to words.

☆ Use cutouts or stickers as manipulative materials.

General Applications for Math

Mathematics is a symbolic language. To successfully perform the operations that are the basis for the early childhood mathematics curriculum, a child must first become fluent in the language of the subject. As with reading, repetition will help children to learn numbers and symbols. Pocket charts are an ideal way to introduce and review math ideas. Teaching mathematics with a pocket chart allows children to become actively involved: They speak the language and perform the operations along with the rest of their class in a risk-free environment that is engaging on a variety of levels. The use of songs and poems in teaching math can be a great help in fostering the sense that math is fun.

Here are some other tips to keep in mind when teaching math with pocket charts:

☆ Number the pockets to teach odd and even.

☆ Introduce graphing by classifying pictures cut out of magazines.

☆ Make your own 1–100 chart by writing numbers on pieces of sentence strips. Vary the colors systematically to teach multiples. Remove different numbers each day and have children find the missing number.

☆ If possible, vary colors of sentence strips to create patterns.

☆ For easy access while teaching a lesson, store small manipulative materials in pockets.

☆ When teaching a math concept, set up an independent center to reinforce skills learned.

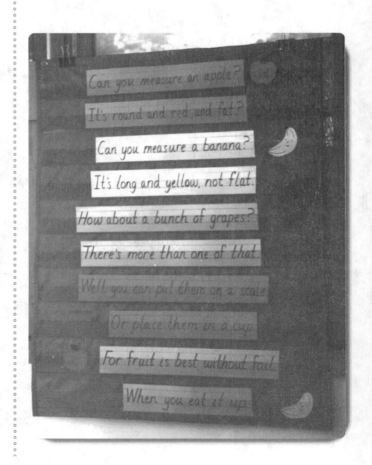

8

How to Use This Book

When reading the individual lesson plans in this book, keep the following thoughts in mind.

☆ When the heading "Pocket Chart Words" appears, you are to copy the text onto sentence strips. It is important to copy the words as they appear; do not break up or consolidate lines.

☆ All the lessons in this book require simple advance preparation. This preparation generally takes only a few minutes. If you do not have easy access to a copy machine, consider making a list of the copies you will need for several lessons and copying them at one time. (Or, simply use an overhead projector to trace the templates onto colored tag.)

☆ Advance preparation also includes gluing the copies onto tagboard, so be sure to allow time for the glue to dry.

Resources for Pocket Chart Supplies

The basic materials needed to complete the lessons in this book are available at most teaching supply stores. They can also be obtained through the companies listed below.

Teaching Resource Center Catalog
 (1-800-833-3389)

American Academic Supplies
(1-800-325-9118)

Beckley-Cardy
(1-800-227-1178)

More Resources for Poems and Math

Because teaching with pocket charts is so much fun, you will eventually seek new sources of ideas for lessons. The books listed below are full of poems, lessons, and math activities.

Graphing Across the Curriculum by Tina Cohen and Valerie Williams (Scholastic, 1995)

The Pocket Chart Book by Valerie SchifferDanoff (Scholastic, 1996)

Pocket Charts for Emergent Readers by Valerie SchifferDanoff (Scholastic, 1997)

Scholastic Integrated Language Arts Resource Book by Valerie SchifferDanoff (Scholastic, 1995)

Thematic Poems, Songs, and Fingerplays by Meish Goldish (Scholastic, 1993)

NUMBER SENSE AND NUMERATION

Understanding Number Meaning

Understanding numbers helps children make sense of our world. Numbers are used to quantify, locate, identify, name, and measure everything from money to ingredients in a recipe. Giving children a variety of experiences with numbers will help them to see that mastering numbers is essential and can be fun.

11

Teddy Bear Count

PURPOSE

To name and count the numbers 1–10 and recognize one-to-one correspondence.

MATERIALS

☆ 34" x 42" pocket chart
☆ 10 teddy bear templates (page 20)
☆ 6 sentence strips
☆ scissors
☆ glue
☆ tagboard
☆ crayons or markers

SETUP

1 Write each line of the poem on a separate sentence strip.

2 Copy, color, and glue teddy bears onto tagboard. When the glue is dry, cut out the bears.

Pocket Chart Sentence Strips

(Please note that wherever a word for a number appears in the poem, you should write the numeral above it.)

One, two, three and four

You can count even more.

Five, six, seven and eight

Teddy bears stand up straight.

Here are nine and ten.

Let's count the teddy bears again!

LESSON

1 Place one teddy bear at a time in the chart. Ask children, "What do you see?" or "How many teddy bears do you see now?" as you increase the number of teddy bears in the chart.

2 One by one, count the teddy bears as you take them out of the chart and hand them to different children in the class.

3 Tell children, "We're going to put the teddy bears in a poem now." Place the first line of the poem in the chart and read it with children. Then ask, "How many teddy bears can we place with this line of the poem?" Once children have responded, have four children place the teddy bears in the chart. Continue this

process until the poem is complete and the correct number of teddy bears have been added to the chart.

4 For the last line of the poem, "Let's count again," recount teddy bears in the chart, pointing to numbers above the words as you do so.

5 Hand out teddy bears to another set of children. Have the class chant the poem together, and allow a new set of children to place the teddy bears in the chart.

Follow-Up Activities

☆ Extend this lesson by assigning ten different children the role of a numbered teddy bear and asking them to come up to the chart at the appropriate time.

☆ Ask children, "What else can we use to count to ten?" Responses may include: fingers, toes, or items in the room. Then have children count to ten using manipulative materials.

☆ Allow children to go on a number hunt to find items in the room that come in multiples of 2, 5, and 10.

☆ Have each child choose a number from 1–10 and write it on a slip of paper. Then circulate with a bag of small manipulative materials and count out the correct number of items for each child as the class counts along.

Literature Link

One Smiling Grandma: A Caribbean Counting Book by Ann Marie Linden (Penguin, 1992)

Ten Little Ducks by Franklin Hammond (Scholastic, 1987)

Ten, Nine, Eight by Molly Bang (Penguin, 1983)

Ten Teddy Bears All in a Row

PURPOSE

To develop the meaning of cardinal and ordinal numbers.

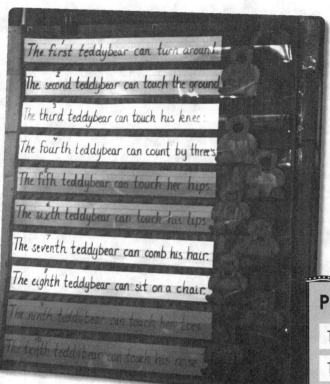

MATERIALS

☆ 34" x 42" pocket chart
☆ 10 teddy bear templates (page 20)
☆ 10 sentence strips
   (optional: assorted colors)
☆ tagboard or construction paper
☆ scissors
☆ glue
☆ crayons or markers

SETUP

1 Write the poem on sentence strips. (If you are using several colors of sentence strips, use one color per couplet. This color pattern will emphasize the rhyme scheme of the poem. As a language extension, you might ask the class for other words that rhyme with the last word in each line.

2 Make ten copies of the teddy bear template, color them, and glue onto the tagboard. When the glue is dry, cut out the bears.

3 Place the ten teddy bears in the pocket chart in a row going down the side of the chart, one in each pocket.

LESSON

1 Count the teddy bears with the children to review counting to ten.

Pocket Chart Sentence Strips

The first teddy bear can turn around.

The second teddy bear can touch the ground.

The third teddy bear can touch his knees.

The fourth teddy bear can count by threes.

The fifth teddy bear can touch her hips.

The sixth teddy bear can touch his lips.

The seventh teddy bear can comb his hair.

The eighth teddy bear can sit on a chair.

The ninth teddy bear can touch her toes.

The tenth teddy bear can touch her nose.

by Valerie SchifferDanoff

2 Tell children that in this poem each of the teddy bears is doing something different. Children may recognize the similarity between this poem and "Teddy bear, teddy bear, turn around."

3 Take the first sentence strip and place it in the chart in the same pocket as the first teddy bear, reciting the line at the same time.

4 Continue until the whole poem is in the chart. For younger children, work on four or six lines at a time. If you are using different colors, point out the patterns made by the strips. Ask the class if they notice any words that rhyme.

5 Read the poem with the class again, and allow children to perform the actions for each teddy bear.

6 Ask children questions based on the poem, such as "Which teddy bear can turn around?" Ask a volunteer to come up to the chart, count to find the correct teddy bear, and point to show the class the correct answer.

7 As an alternative to the previous step, ask children "Do you know what the first teddy bear is doing?" Ask a volunteer to come up to the chart and point to and read the answer.

Follow-Up Activities

☆ Assign different children the roles of the first teddy bear, the second teddy bear, and so on, and ask them to perform the correct action while you read the poem.

☆ For individual reinforcement:

1. Reduce and copy the teddy bear template, making ten bears for each child in the class.

2. Children can then color, cut out and glue teddy bears onto an appropriately sized strip of paper.

3. Ask children to point to the first teddy bear, the second teddy bear, and so on.

4. Then direct children to write the number above each teddy bear.

5. Direct children to color the bow on each teddy bear a different color; for example, "Color the bow on the *first* teddy bear red." Older children can write a sentence about each of the teddy bears.

☆ Make a class big book about the teddy bears. Together, write sentences for example, "The first teddy bear is brown," and "The second teddy bear is blue." Keep the book on display and use it when you repeat this lesson.

Literature Link

The April Rabbits by David Cleveland (Coward, McCann & Geoghegan, Inc.1978)

Teddy Bear, Teddy Bear by Kathleen Hague (Scholastic, 1991)

Golden Bear by Ruth Young (Penguin, 1992)

Fruit in the Fridge

PURPOSE

To count and to explore number relationships.

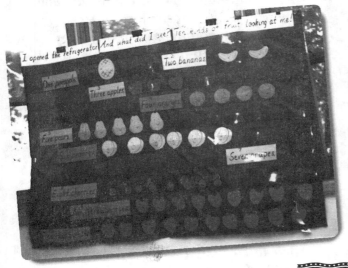

MATERIALS

☆ 34" x 42" pocket chart (If you have access to a larger pocket chart, this lesson would benefit from the added space.)

☆ small clamp clips or pushpins

☆ 12–14 sentence strips (optional: assorted colors)

☆ fruit templates: 1 pineapple, 2 bananas, 3 apples, 4 oranges, 5 pears, 6 peaches, 7 grapes, 8 cherries, 9 strawberries, 10 raspberries (pages 21–25)

☆ tagboard or construction paper

☆ markers or crayons

☆ scissors

☆ glue

"Our Class Refrigerator" option:

two pieces of 22" x 28" posterboard, 5–6 feet of self-adhesive Velcro, heavy packing tape

SETUP

1 Copy, color, and glue onto tagboard the correct number of the various kinds of fruit specified in the poem. When they are dry, cut them out.

2 Write the poem on sentence strips. If possible, use colors that match the fruit; for example, orange paper for "four oranges" and yellow paper for "two bananas."

3 Place the first two lines of the poem across the top of the pocket chart, secured against the wall with pushpins or attached to the chart with clamp clips.

"Our Class Refrigerator" Option:

Make the two pieces of white tagboard into a refrigerator by joining them length-wise with

Pocket Chart Sentence Strips

I opened the refrigerator and what did I see?

Ten kinds of fruit smiling at me.

One pineapple,

Two bananas,

Three apples,

Four oranges,

Five pears,

Six peaches,

Seven grapes,

Eight cherries,

Nine strawberries,

Ten raspberries.

by Valerie SchifferDanoff

packing tape or filament tape. Attach one side of Velcro in horizontal rows across each piece of tagboard to look like shelves in a refrigerator. Attach the other side of the Velcro to fruits. The board can be labeled "Our Class Refrigerator." This can then be clipped to the bottom of the chart or tacked to the wall. It can also stand on the floor without extra support. This refrigerator can be used to hold the extra fruit until it comes up in the poem.

LESSON

1 Ask the class what kinds of things they have in their refrigerator. Then tell them, "We're going to turn this pocket chart into our own little refrigerator to count different kinds of fruit."

2 Hand out the fruit in complete groups; for example, three apples to one child or five pears to another. Explain that when the line describing their fruit is read, they must come up to the pocket chart and "put the fruit away in its proper place."

3 Read the first two lines of the poem: "I opened the refrigerator and what did I see? Ten kinds of fruit smiling at me."

4 Read the rest of the poem line by line, stopping after each line to allow children to place the correct number of fruit in the correct spot in the refrigerator. With the class, count each fruit aloud.

5 Once all the fruit is in the "refrigerator," count each kind of fruit a second time.

6 Help children explore number relationships by asking the following questions.

☆ Which kind of fruit has more than one? More than two? More than three?

☆ Do we have an even or odd number of apples? Of cherries?

☆ Which kind of fruit has one less than three? One less than four?

☆ Which kind of fruit has one less than eight but more than five?

Follow-Up Activities

☆ Count the total number of fruit in the refrigerator.

☆ Remove the fruit from the refrigerator. Hand out single pieces of fruit to children in the class. Ask all of the "apples" to come up to the front of the class so that the class can count the fruit as a group. Do this for each kind of fruit.

☆ Children can make individual "Refrigerator Books" simply by folding several sheets of white paper in half and stapling on the fold. Children can draw any food item they like to represent each number on a page; for example, page one could have one egg, page two could have two cartons of milk.

☆ Make a class big book title "Fruit in the Fridge." Have children work in pairs to draw their own versions of the fruit pictured in the poem. Allow the class to use the pocket chart as a reference.

☆ Make a fruit salad. Assign each child in the class a fruit to bring to school. Discuss the size of the fruit with the class. For example, one pineapple will feed many people, but one cherry will not.

Literature Link

Eating the Alphabet by Lois Ehlert (Harcourt Brace Jovanovich, 1989)

One Hundred Is a Family by Pam Muñoz Ryan (Hyperion, 1994)

Counting Rhymes compiled by John Foster (Oxford Press, 1997)

The One-Hundredth Day

PURPOSE

To skip count and celebrate the hundredth day of school.

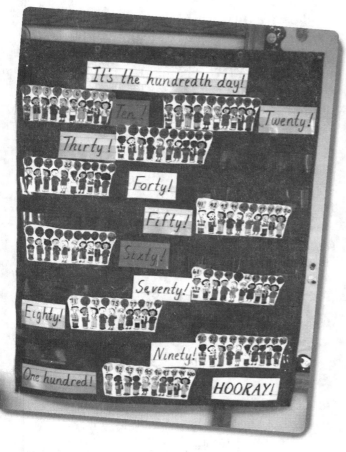

MATERIALS

☆ 34" x 42" pocket chart

☆ 10 of the group of children with balloons (page 26)

☆ 12 sentence strips (optional: various colors)

☆ scissors

☆ glue

☆ tagboard

☆ markers or crayons

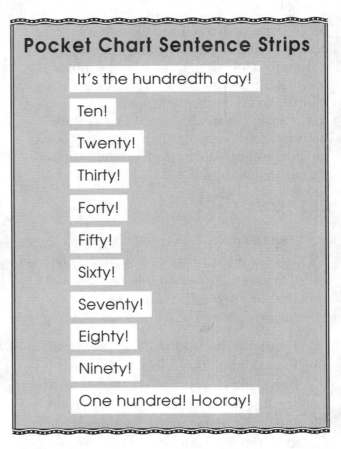

Pocket Chart Sentence Strips

It's the hundredth day!

Ten!

Twenty!

Thirty!

Forty!

Fifty!

Sixty!

Seventy!

Eighty!

Ninety!

One hundred! Hooray!

SETUP

1 Write the words on sentence strips.

2 Make ten copies of the template of the children with balloons. Color them and glue onto tagboard. When the glue is dry, cut them out. You may choose to color the balloons in a pattern as well.

LESSON

1 Tell children, "Instead of counting by ones we are going to skip count, but you have to figure out the number we are using to skip count by."

2 Place the words and groups of ten children in the chart as you read the poem. Ask children, "By what number are we skip counting?"

3 Hand out the number words and groups of ten to various children. Repeat the poem. Have the child holding the correct word come up as the number is read. When the poem is finished, have the children holding the cutouts of the groups of ten come up one by one as the class counts off by ten.

Follow-Up Activities

☆ Create new number sets by cutting apart the groups of ten, and try skip counting by twos, fours, or fives.

☆ Ask your children to group items by tens. You can use crayons, pennies, or pieces of paper.

☆ Make a class book using ten copies of the template. Paste them onto large sheets of paper and number each balloon from one to one hundred.

Literature Link

One Hundred Is a Family by Pam Muñoz Ryan.(Hyperion Books, 1994)

From One to One Hundred by Teri Sloat (Penguin, 1991)

Teddy Bear Templates

Copy 10 bears.

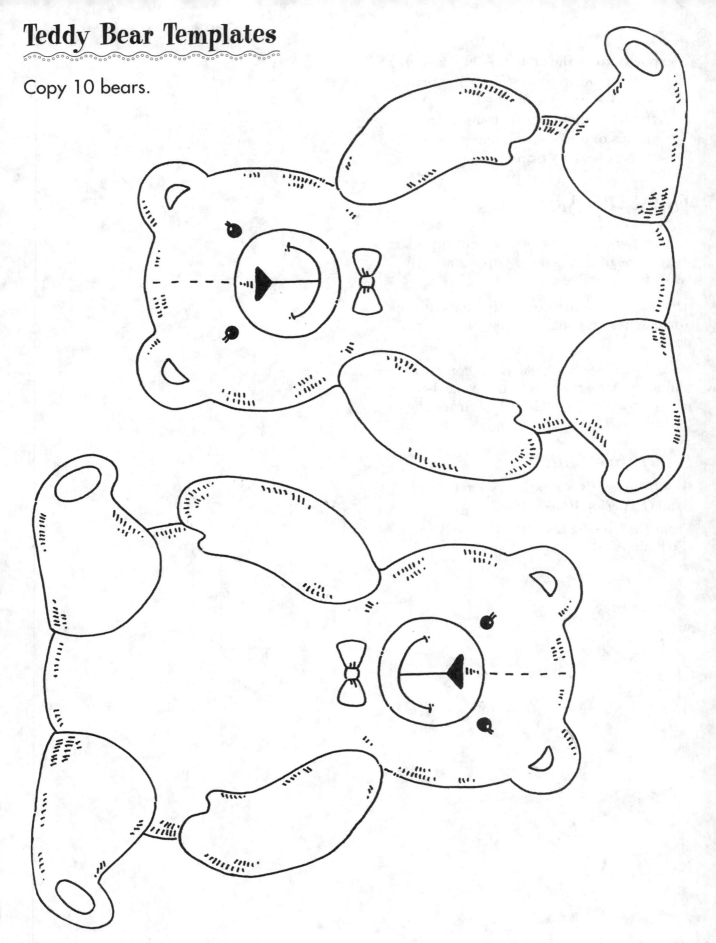

Fruit Templates

Copy the fruit.

Fruit Templates

Pocket Charts for Math Scholastic Professional Books

Fruit Templates

Fruit Templates

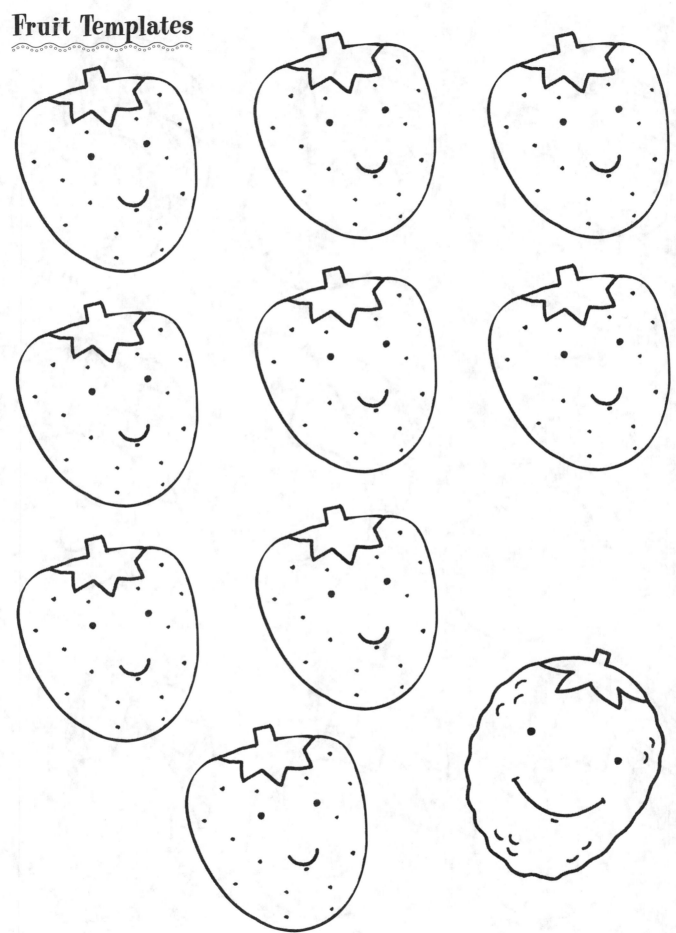

Fruit Templates

100th-Day Children Template

Copy 10 of the group
of children.

CONCEPTS OF
WHOLE NUMBER OPERATIONS

Understanding and Applying Fundamental Operations

Using real objects to count and solve problems can help children to develop a better understanding of the four basic operations, and apply this knowledge to situations in the real world. Helping children to develop a good "math sense" enables them to think critically about the process underlying their computations, which in turn lays the groundwork for more complex math skills. To experience the meaning of operations, it helps to focus on concepts and relationships in addition to written computation, and the pocket chart is the ideal way to present this foundation material.

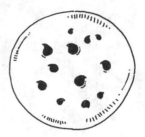

Ten Red Apples

PURPOSE
To recognize sets.

MATERIALS
☆ 34" x 42" pocket chart
☆ 6 sentence strips
☆ tree template (page 34)
☆ 10 apple templates (page 35)
☆ 2 feet self-adhesive Velcro
☆ scissors
☆ markers or crayons
☆ glue
☆ red, brown, green tagboard

Pocket Chart Sentence Strips

Ten red apples growing on a tree,

Five for you and five for me.

Help me shake the tree just so,

Ten red apples fall down below.

One, two, three, four, five,

Six, seven, eight, nine, ten.

SETUP

1 Write the poem on sentence strips.

2 Use the apple template to trace and cut ten apples from the red tagboard.

3 Enlarge and copy the tree template. Cut the treetop from the green tagboard and the trunk from the brown tagboard. Glue the treetop to the trunk.

4 Cut small pieces of Velcro. Attach one side to each of the apples. Attach each of the remaining pieces to the treetop, leaving space between them.

5 Place the sentence strips in the pocket chart. Hang the tree from the pocket chart with small clamps, or use pushpins to display it nearby.

LESSON

1 Read the poem with children.

2 Reread the first two lines of the poem.

3 Invite two children to each take five apples off the tree.

4 Continue reading the poem. When you reach the lines that count from one to five, have the class count with you as the first child puts the apples into pockets on one side of the tree. As you read the line that counts from six to ten, have the second child put the apples into pockets along the other side of the tree.

5 With the class, discuss that these are two sets of five. Ask children what else they can think of that comes in two sets of five, such as fingers and toes.

Follow-Up Activities

☆ Extend this lesson by inviting ten children up to pretend to be the apples and act out the poem as the class recites it. Repeat this activity until all children have had a turn.

☆ Invite five children up. Ask the class how many apples you should give each child so that they all have the same amount. After children have volunteered answers, solve the problem by handing out the apples.

☆ Divide the class into pairs and give each pair ten Unifix cubes or other manipulative materials. Recite the poem and instruct each pair to pretend the manipulative materials are the apples. Then instruct each pair to make two sets of five. When a pair has successfully done this, ask them to try to make five sets of two.

☆ Give each child a sheet of paper. Ask the class to draw an apple tree with ten apples on it. Have them circle five apples with one color crayon and five apples with another color crayon. On the back, have children fold the paper in half and draw five apples on each half of the paper.

Literature Extensions

The Apple Pie Tree by Zoe Hall (Scholastic, 1996)

Two of Everything by Lily Toy Hong (Albert Whitman & Co., 1993)

Five Little Birds

PURPOSE

To recognize, experience, and apply the operation of subtraction.

MATERIALS

☆ 34" x 42" pocket chart
☆ 5 bird templates (page 36)
☆ 12 sentence strips (optional: 2 different colors)
☆ scissors
☆ glue
☆ tagboard or construction paper
☆ markers or crayons

Pocket Chart Sentence Strips

Five little birds peeping at the door,

On flew away and that left four.

Four little birds sitting on a tree,

One flew away and that left three.

Three little birds looking at you,

One flew away and that left two.

Two little birds sitting in the sun,

One flew away and that left one.

One little bird left all alone,

It flew away and that left none.

SETUP

1. Write the poem on sentence strips.

2. Cut pieces of blank sentence strips large enough to cover up the following number words from the second, fourth, sixth, eight, and tenth lines of the poem: four, three, two, one, and none.

3. Make five copies of the bird template, color them, and glue them to the tagboard. When dry, cut them out.

4. Place the lines of the poem in the chart. Cover up the number words with the blank pieces of sentence strip.

5. Place the birds in a vertical row on the chart.

LESSON

1 Children will easily catch the rhyming hint as the poem is read. Read the poem, allowing time for the class to call out the correct number word. When the correct word has been called out, remove the blank piece of sentence strip and say the word.

2 After you have read the poem through once, begin again. Read the first two lines and ask, "How many birds should I remove from the chart now?" Choose a volunteer to remove one bird. Continue the poem, stopping every two lines and repeating the question.

3 Once three birds have been removed, ask: "Are there more birds in the chart or off the chart? How many birds were there in the chart when we began? How many birds flew away? How many birds are left?"

4 Continue and complete the poem.

5 Ask, "What did we do with the birds?" When a child answers that you took them away, you can explain that you have been subtracting the birds from the chart.

Follow-Up Activities

☆ Focus on children's operation sense and the relationship between addition and subtraction by adding extending the poem. Say: "I put some birdseed out. One by one the birds returned. Help me count the birds as they return." Call the children who are holding the birds up to the front. Describe how the birds returned by telling a story such as the following: "First the one by the door returned. Now she's lonely. Oh, here comes the one sitting in the tree. Now how many birds have returned? How many birds are still

away?" Continue until all five birds are returned to the chart. Then repeat the original poem.

☆ Have five children pretend to be the birds and fly away as the class recites the poem. Then have the birds return, one by one.

☆ Recite the following poem. One child stands up as the poem is chanted and, at the appropriate time, chooses a friend. The game continues until the whole class is standing.

There was one little bird in the one little
*   tree,*
"I'm so alone, I need a friend," said she.
So she flew far away over the sea
And brought back a friend to live in the tree.

Now there were two little birds in the
*   one little tree.*
"We're so alone, we need some company."
So they flew far away over the sea
And brought back a friend to live in
*   the tree.*

Now there are three little birds in the one
*   little tree,*
"We're so alone, we need some company…"
and so on.

☆ Extend this lesson by having children draw their own tree. Use Unifix cubes or another small manipulative material to represent the birds. Have children each put five "birds" in their tree. While you read the poem, children can remove a bird at the correct line.

Literature Extensions

Five Little Ducks illustrated by José Aruego (Crown Press, 1989)

Ten out of Bed by Penny Dale (Candlewick Press, 1993)

Ten on a Train: A Countdown Book by John O'Leary (Penguin, 1995)

Cookie Count

PURPOSE

To recognize that objects and counting can be used to solve the problem of equalizing.

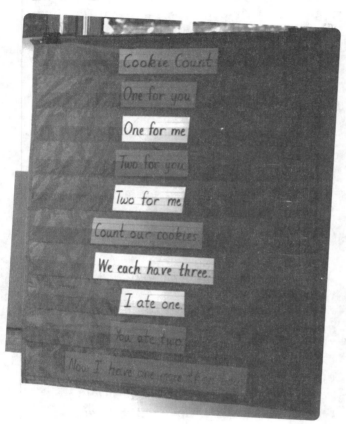

MATERIALS

☆ 34" x 42" pocket chart
☆ 5–10 sentence strips
☆ 6 cookie templates (page 37)
☆ crayons or markers
☆ glue
☆ tagboard or construction paper

SETUP

1 Write words on sentence strips and place them in the chart.

2 Copy the cookie template so that you have six cookies. Color and glue onto tagboard. When the glue is dry, cut around the outlines of the cookies.

Pocket Chart Sentence Strips

Cookie Count

One for you,

One for me,

Two for you,

Two for me.

Count our cookies.

We each have three.

I ate one.

You ate two.

Now I have one more than you.

by Valerie SchifferDanoff

LESSON

1 Ask children to try to estimate how many cookies there are in the poem.

2 Read the poem.

3 Ask the question again. (You might suggest looking for the words that represent numbers.)

4 Read the poem placing cookies in the chart for each of the first four lines. Stop when you get to "We each have three," and ask children, "How many cookies do you think will be left at the end of the poem?"

5 Continue reading. Invite two children up to "eat the cookies" as indicated in the poem.

6 Ask: "Did each child get an equal number of cookies? Did each child have the same number of cookies left at the end of the poem?" Children should be able to answer by looking at the number of cookies left.

Hands-On and Follow-Up Activities

☆ The best follow-up for this one is to have real cookies. If possible, splurge and buy a bag or two of animal crackers or other small cookies for the class. Pair the children and read the poem aloud, giving them time to manipulate their own cookies as indicated in the poem.

☆ Reinforce the concept of subtraction by increasing the number of cookies used. Include both odd and even numbers.

☆ Once the cookies have been eaten, continue this lesson by having pairs of children work with other manipulative materials.

Literature Extensions

Cookie Count by Robert Sabuda (Simon & Schuster, 1997)

If You Give a Mouse a Cookie by Laura Joffe Numeroff (HarperCollins, 1987)

Apple Tree Template

Copy the tree at 200% onto 11" x 17" paper. (This is half size.)

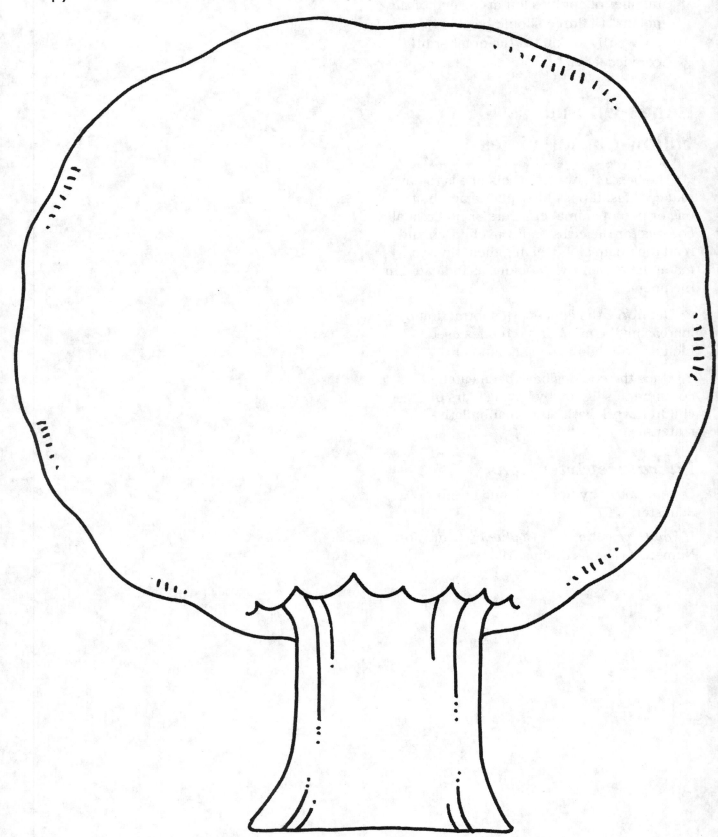

Apple Templates

Copy 10 apples.

Bird Template

Copy 5 birds.

Cookie Template

Copy 6 cookies.

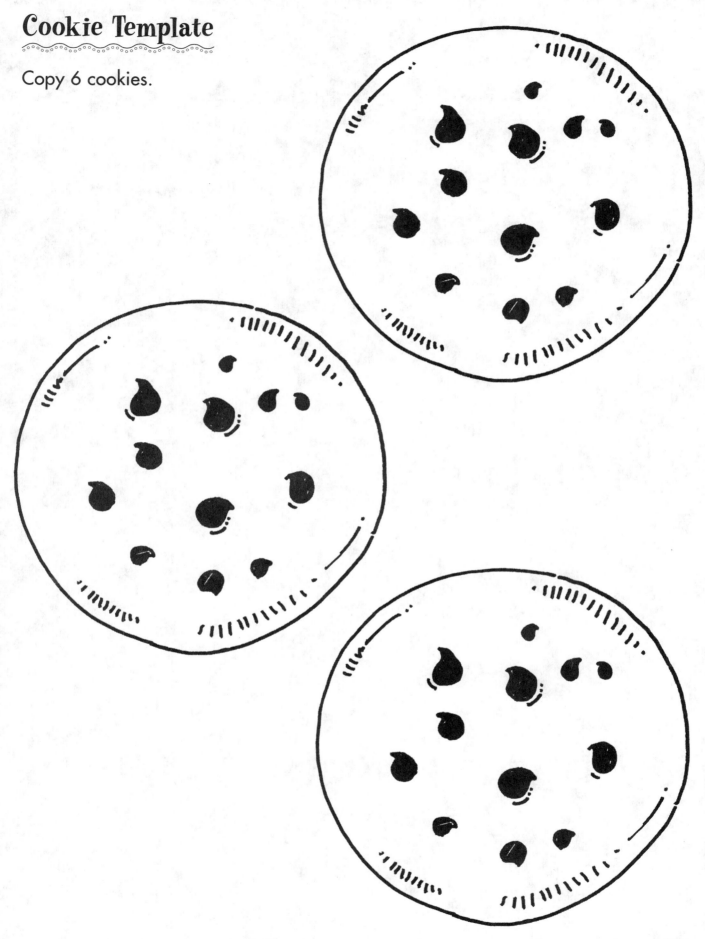

GEOMETRY

Spatial Understandings for Interpreting and Appreciating Our Geometric World

Geometry helps us to represent and describe our world in an orderly manner. Children see basic shapes all around them in their classroom, their home, and in nature. Most children begin to appreciate geometry at a very young age through the use of building blocks. With this early start, you can make the inevitable connection between geometry and a fun activity and make it an exciting teaching experience. Beginning geometry teaches children how to explore, draw, and compare everyday objects, and develop an understanding of the geometric relationships in our world.

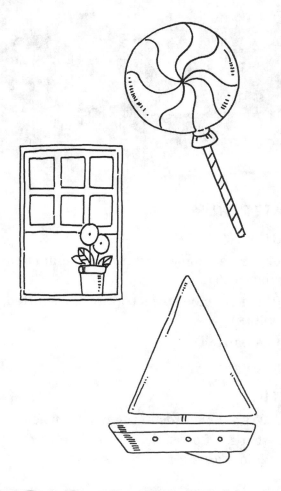

Draw a...

PURPOSE

To recognize and name shapes and their attributes.

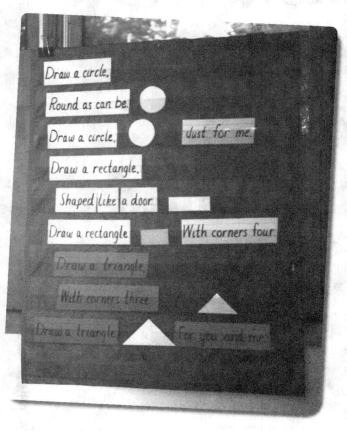

MATERIALS

☆ 34" x 42" pocket chart

☆ circle, rectangle, and triangle templates (pages 46)

☆ 9–12 sentence strips (optional: assorted colors)

☆ tagboard

☆ scissors

SETUP

1 Write the words of the poem on sentence strips. (If possible, use three different colors, one for each shape.)

Pocket Chart Sentence Strips

Draw a circle, Round as can be.

Draw a circle, Just for me.

Draw a rectangle, Shaped like a door.

Draw a rectangle, With corners four.

Draw a triangle, With corners three.

Draw a triangle, For you and me.

2 Using the templates, copy, trace, and cut shapes in various sizes from tagboard. (The templates can be enlarged or reduced using a copy machine.) If you are using colored sentence strips, use construction paper for the shapes that match the colors of the sentence strips. You can also prepare colored shapes with your class as a pre-lesson activity. To do this, copy the shape template so that each child can have one. Pass them out, and ask children to color each shape in a color to match the sentence strips you used for that shape in the poem. Then ask the children to cut out their shapes.

3 Place the words of the poem in the chart. Place all the shapes in the last pockets at the bottom of the chart.

LESSON

1 Read the lines about the circle. Invite a child to choose a circle from the shapes at the bottom of the chart and place it next to the lines about the circle.

2 Continue until the whole poem has been read and all the shapes identified in the poem have been matched with a cutout shape. You will have some cutouts left at the bottom of the chart.

3 Reread the poem while tracing the shapes with you hands. Model this for the children to mimic. The same can be done by "tracing" shapes with your head. Try it at home first in front of a mirror. Children will really enjoy this.

4 Reread the poem, pausing at each line to call children up to place the correct shape next to the line you have read.

Follow-Up Activities

☆ Remove all the shapes from the chart. If you have not asked children to make their own shapes earlier, hand out the shapes from the pocket chart. Then say the lines of the poem, instructing children to stand and hold their shape in the air when it is mentioned.

☆ Older children can trace shapes from a cardboard pattern, cut them out, and then glue onto paper to make a collage. For younger children, distribute precut shapes in various sizes and colors that they can glue for their collages. This art activity will reinforce the attributes of the various shapes.

☆ Hand out tag shapes. Have children be shape detectives while they try to match their shape to shapes in the room.

☆ Read or write the following poem, place it in the chart, and have children perform the actions of marching, playing horns and drums, and roaring like a lion. Ask children to trace with their hands the shape that is named when each line is read. You can also substitute other shapes for the circle.

Make-Believe Parade

After a circle
We had made,
We marched around
In a big parade.
With our make-believe
Horns and drums in hand,
We all pretended
To be a band.
And then we pretended
A circus ring—
I was a lion!
I was a king.
— Leland B. Jacobs, from *Poetry Place Anthology* (Scholastic, 1990)

Literature Link

Shapes by Anne Geddes (Cedco, 1997)

Shape Space by Cathryn Falwek (Clarion Books, 1992)

It Can Be...

PURPOSE

To recognize and represent the shapes we see.

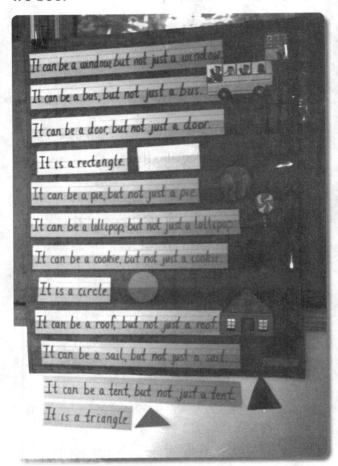

MATERIALS

☆ 34" x 42" Pocket Chart

☆ shape templates (page 46)

☆ shape pictures (page 47–49)

☆ 12 sentence strips (optional: 3 different colors)

☆ scissors

☆ glue

☆ construction paper

☆ tagboard

☆ markers or crayons

Pocket Chart Sentence Strips

This chart is a play on the story It Looked Like Spilt Milk *by Charles G. Shaw, (HarperCollins, 1947)*

It can be a window, but not just a window.
It can be a bus, but not just a bus.
It can be a door, but not just a door.
It is a rectangle.
It can be a pie, but not just a pie.
It can be a lollipop, but not just a lollipop.
It can be a cookie, but not just a cookie.
It is a circle.
It can be a roof, but not just a roof.
It can be a sail, but not just a sail.
It can be a tent, but not just a tent.
It is a triangle.

SETUP

1 Write the words of the poem on sentence strips. If you are using different colors, write the lines for each shape on matching-colored sentence strips.

2 Trace and cut shapes on tag.

3 Copy, color, and cut out shape pictures.

4 Place the first three sentences of each stanza and the object pictures for each shape in the pocket chart. Skip a pocket between each stanza so that later you can insert the line that identifies each shape. Place the last sentence and the

plain shapes at the bottom of the chart or in your lap so that they are accessible while reading the poem.

LESSON

1 Read the shape sentences of the first stanza to the children. Review the attributes of the objects shown. For example, point out that the window has four sides, two one length and two another length. When you have reviewed each of the three objects shown, invite a child to match the correct sentence and shape.

2 Follow the above process until you have finished the poem.

3 Ask children, "What else looks like a triangle (circle, rectangle)?"

Follow-Up Activities

☆ Brainstorm other things in our environment that are made up of these shapes and add them to the chart.

☆ Go on a shape walk around the school or community, searching for shapes in your environment. Walk around a baseball diamond, point out the shape of a clock face, examine the tabletop where the children eat lunch. What shapes do they see?

☆ Make shape pictures. At each table have at least one of each shape template for each child. Direct children to trace the shape onto their paper. Then they can draw inside and around it to represent something in their world. Children can copy ideas from the chart such as the bus or the tent, or use their own ideas. For younger children, use precut shapes.

☆ Create a "Shapes in Our World" mural. Have students glue the artwork generated in the previous activity onto mural-size paper.

Literature Link

Color Zoo by Lois Ehlert (HarperCollins, 1984)

The Secret Birthday Message by Eric Carle (Harper Trophy, 1986)

The Shape of Things by Dayle Ann Dodds (Candlewick Press, 1994)

Shapes for a Heart

PURPOSE

To divide and combine shapes to create new shapes and to follow directions.

MATERIALS

☆ 34" x 42" pocket chart

☆ 8 sentence strips

☆ circle and square templates (page 50)

☆ tagboard

☆ 2 sheets of 12" x 18" construction paper for each child in class

☆ scissors

☆ markers or crayons

☆ glue

SETUP

1 Write the pocket chart words on sentence strips. Place the title and steps 1 through 5 in chart. Turn steps 3, 4, and 5 facedown.

2 Make enough copies of the template squares and circles so that children can work in pairs.

3 Make a complete paper heart and glue it onto the rectangle. Compile the components of a second heart (the square and the divided circle) but leave them separate.

4 Have all the materials needed to make the hearts at children's places. Put the rectangles in front of each child like place mats.

LESSON

1 Hold up the rectangle and review its attributes. Repeat with the square and the circle. Ask children to look at their own circle and square templates.

Pocket Chart Sentence Strips

Shapes for a Heart

1. Trace and cut out a square.

2. Trace and cut out a circle.

3. Fold the circle in half.

   Unfold and cut on fold.

4. Glue the square onto the rectangle paper

   with one corner pointing to you.

5. Place and glue half-circles along top sides

   of square to meet at the corner.

44

2 Explain that there are directions on the chart that the class is going to follow. The directions show how to divide and combine these two shapes to form a heart.

3 Read steps 1 and 2 with children. Then allow children time to cut out a circle and a square.

4 Give children a few minutes to move the shapes around on the paper. Point out that the circle fits inside the square.

5 Turn over step 3. Read it aloud and allow children time to divide the circle. At this point, ask children if they know how these pieces can be used to form a heart. Then follow with step 4.

6 Read step 5, and give children time to glue their half circles to the square.

7 Use your whole model to review how the square and circle became a heart, folding down half circles to make the heart back into a square.

Follow-Up Activities

☆ Allow children time to experiment with more folding and cutting of shapes. First, see if they can figure out how to make the square into triangles (by folding diagonally) and rectangles (by folding in half).

☆ Brainstorm a list of foods that come in particular shapes. Consider pizza: a circle that is broken up into triangles. Saltines, which are square, form a rectangle when two are combined side by side. Ask children to bring in foods that form shapes, and have a shape food party.

☆ Give a group of four children a piece of rope tied together at the ends to make a loop. Challenge children to hold the rope to form a square, rectangle or triangle.

Literature Link

Picture Pie by Ed Emberly (Little Brown, 1984)

Shapes for Lunch by Charles Reasoner (Putnam Grosset, 1997)

Shape Templates

Copy each shape.

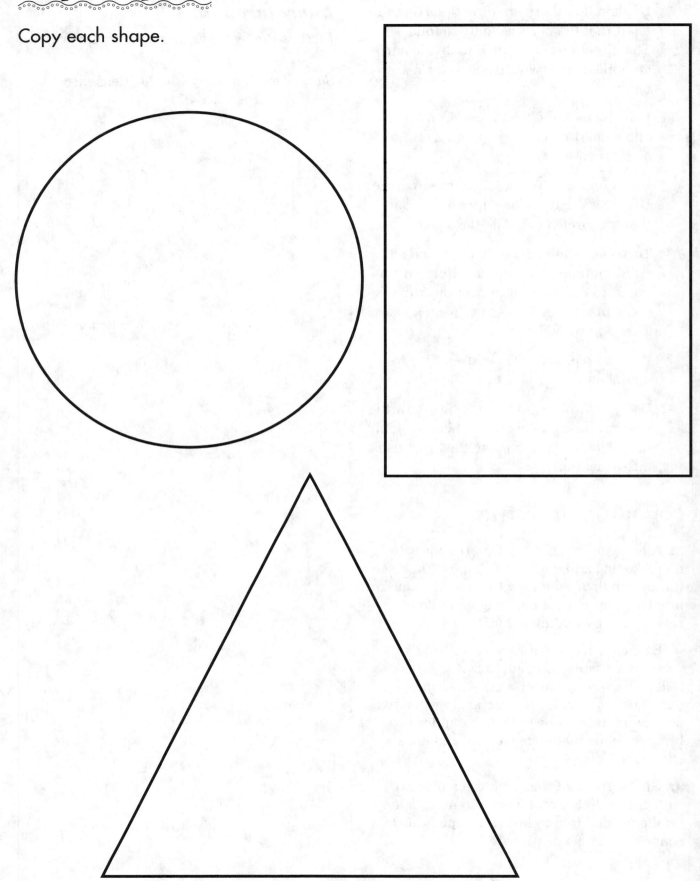

Shape Templates

Copy each object.

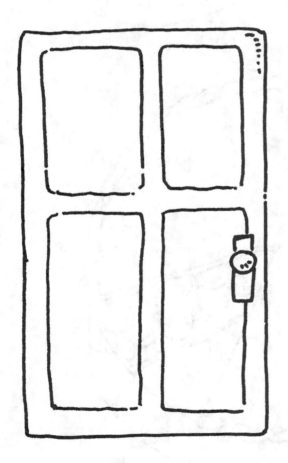

Shape Templates

Copy each object.

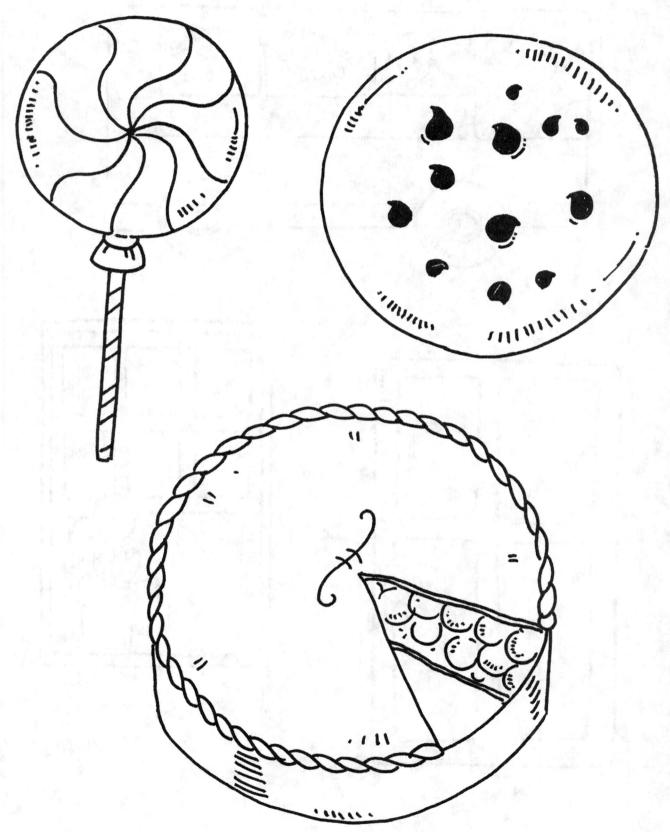

Pocket Charts for Math Scholastic Professional Books

Shape Templates

Copy each object.

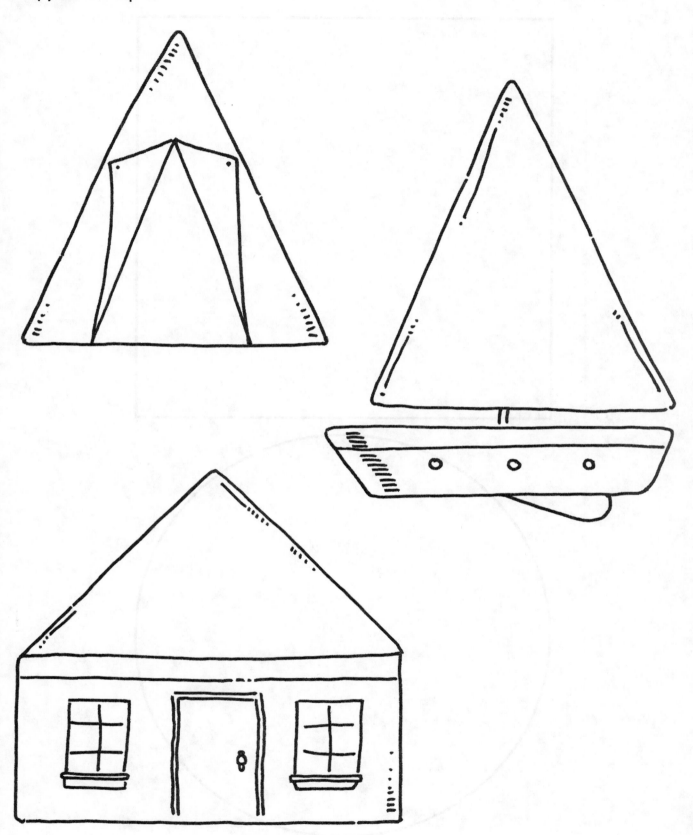

Circle and Square Template

Copy each shape.

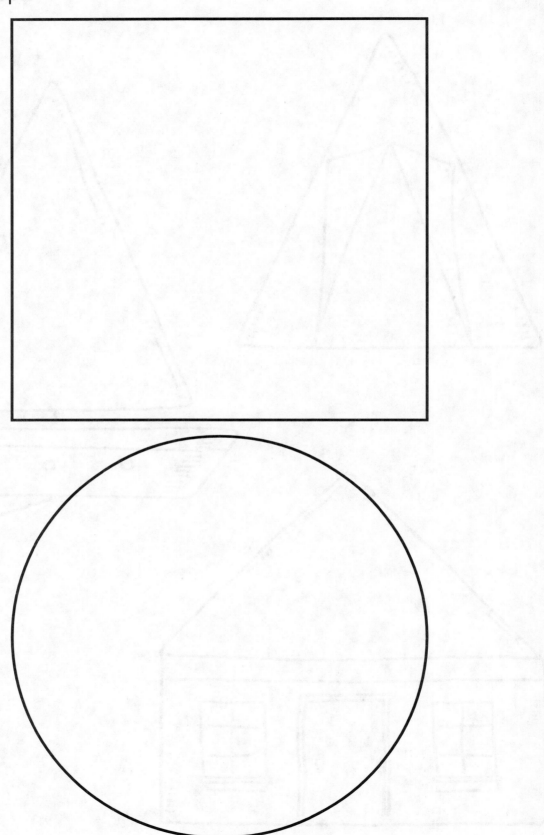

MEASUREMENT

Understanding Attributes and the Process of Measurement

Measurement is an aspect of mathematics that is used every day. Children can see from their own experiences that measurement has a very important function in their lives. To prepare them for more complicated measurement exercises, children need a variety of experiences that focus on comparing objects.

I Am In-Between

PURPOSE
To estimate and compare objects according to their size.

MATERIALS

☆ 34" x 42" pocket chart

☆ 6 sentence strips

☆ Child, baby, adult, ball, door templates (pages 55–56)

☆ tagboard

☆ scissors

☆ glue

☆ markers or crayons

SETUP

1 Write the pocket chart words on sentence strips.

2 Copy and color the door, ball, grown-up, baby, and child templates. Glue the copies onto tagboard, allow them to dry, and then cut out.

3 Place the poem and objects in chart.

Pocket Chart Sentence Strips

The door is tall.

The ball is small.

I am in-between.

Grown-ups are tall.

Babies are small.

I am in-between.

LESSON

1 Read the poem with children.

2 After you have read the poem, compare the objects (door, ball, child, and grown-up, baby, and child) at the bottom of the chart so that children can see the variations in size.

3 Ask several volunteers to come to the front to show how they compare in size to the ball and the door to the classroom.

Follow-Up Activities

☆ Invite children to compare themselves to other objects in the room. Ask, "Can you find things that are bigger than you?" and "Can you find things that are smaller than you?"

☆ Have children take out their book bags. Ask: "What is small enough to fit in your book bag? What is too big to fit in your book bag?"

Literature Link

Blue Sea by Robert Kalan (William Morrow, 1993)

New Shoes for Silvia by Johanna Hurwitz (William Morrow, 1993)

How Can You Measure Fruit?

PURPOSE

To understand that objects have many measurable attributes.

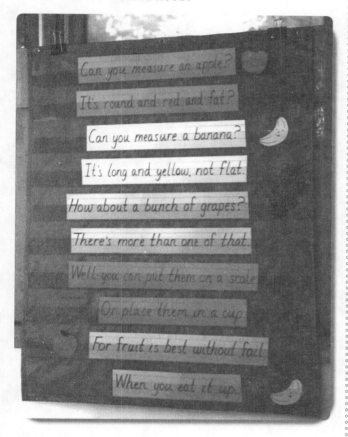

MATERIALS

☆ 34" x 42" pocket chart

☆ 10 sentence strips (optional: 2 of each color)

☆ apple, banana, grapes templates (pages 21 and 23)

☆ tagboard or construction paper

☆ scissors

☆ glue

☆ markers or crayons

Note: Having real fruit available is a good idea.

Pocket Chart Sentence Strips

Can you measure an apple?

It's round and red and fat.

Can you measure a banana?

It's long and yellow, not flat.

How about a bunch of grapes?

There's more than one of that.

Well, you can put them on a scale.

Or place them in a cup.

For fruit is best, without fail,

When you eat it up.

by Valerie SchifferDanoff

SETUP

1 Write pocket chart sentence strips. If you are using different colors, write the first two lines on one color, the second two lines on a different color, and so on.

2 Copy and color the apple, banana, and grapes templates (see pages 21 and 23). Glue the fruit onto tagboard. When the glue is dry, cut out the fruit.

3 Place the sentence strips and fruit in chart.

LESSON

1 Invite children to talk about a trip to the market to buy food. Ask, "Did you ever notice what happens to the fruit and vegetables at the checkout counter?" (A: It gets weighed.) Do not give them the answer if they do not know.

53

2 Read the poem. If you have real fruit available, hold up the appropriate piece as you read.

3 Point out the attributes of the fruits, such as: color, shape, number of pieces, and weight.

4 Invite children to suggest other ways of describing each kind of fruit.

5 Reread the poem. Then discuss measuring other pieces of fruit, such as a pear or an orange. Direct the questions in the poem to the class. Make a list of children's ideas about the new fruit.

Follow-Up Activities

☆ Experiment with some of the children's suggestions for measuring, using real fruit or objects in the room.

☆ Use a balance to compare weights.

☆ Have each child in the class bring in an apple. Use a real scale to compare the weights of the apples.

☆ Give each child a piece of string with which to measure the circumference of the apples.

Literature Link

The Fattest, Tallest, Biggest Snowman Ever by Bettina Ling (Scholastic, 1997)

Is Blue Whale the Biggest Thing There Is? by Robert Wells (Albert Whitman, 1993)

Too Much by Dorothy Stott (E. P. Dutton, 1990)

In-Between Templates

Copy each person and object.

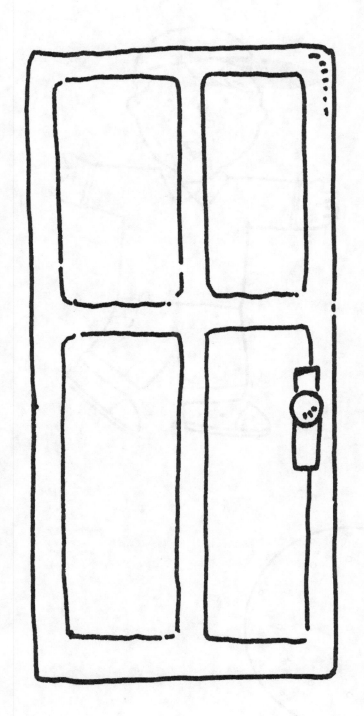

PATTERNS AND RELATIONSHIPS

Understanding Connections by Looking for Patterns

Encouraging children to look for patterns helps them understand how pervasive mathematics concepts are. Everywhere a child looks, from his or her shirt to seashells on the beach, patterns can be found. Representing patterns in a variety of ways helps children form relationships across the mathematical concepts.

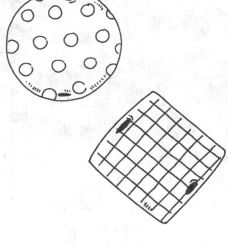

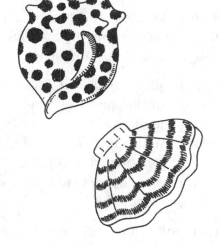

Shapes and Designs

PURPOSE

To identify patterns by attributes such as color, shape, orientation, and size.

MATERIALS

- ☆ 24" x 24" pocket chart
- ☆ 4 sentence strips, 2 of each color (optional)
- ☆ 20 bead templates (page 64)
- ☆ tagboard
- ☆ glue
- ☆ markers or crayons
- ☆ scissors

SETUP

1 Write words on two different-colored sentence strips (if possible) to emphasize end rhymes. That's a pattern, too.

2 Copy the bead template a minimum of five times. Color each different bead with the same colors. For example, use pink and yellow for the round beads, green for the oblong and so on, so that

Pocket Chart Sentence Strips

Shapes and designs

Stars, spots, lines.

Beads all around

Patterns can be found.

by Valerie SchifferDanoff

they can be used in a pattern. Glue the beads onto tag and cut them out. Make a minimum of twenty beads.

3 Place the pocket chart words in the center of the chart. Then display the beads around the words to look like a necklace, being careful to make a pattern of the different beads.

LESSON

1 Children will be very attracted to the display on the chart. Invite them to tell you what they see. Do this briefly, allowing each child to say one thing about the display.

2 Read the poem. See if children recognize the rhyme pattern.

3 Define and discuss the vocabulary you will be using to name the attributes: shape, design, line, spot, stripe.

4 Invite one child to describe the attributes of that particular bead. For example, he or she could describe one bead as round, spotted, and pink and yellow. It is important to discuss these attributes, as they can later be used to identify, extend, and create patterns.

5 Direct children to look closely at the chart. Invite them to identify the patterns made by the beads.

Follow-Up Activities

☆ Have children snap their fingers and clap their hands to highlight the pattern made by the beads.

☆ Give children the opportunity to change the pattern in the chart.

☆ Use manipulative math materials, such as Unifix cubes, to repeat the pattern.

☆ Give each child a set of beads to color and then glue onto tagboard and cut out. Use the beads for a whole-class sorting and patterning activity.

☆ Make enough copies of beads on construction paper for children to cut out and glue their own patterns.

☆ Sort the beads by shape attributes.

☆ Use real beads, which are inexpensive and are available in catalogs. Children can string their own necklaces.

☆ Children can string edible necklaces from colored cereal shaped like circles.

☆ Make beads from Sculpey clay.

☆ Write a Pattern Big Book.

1. White out the pattern on a copy of the bead template and enlarge it on a copy machine.

2. Give each child in the class a copy to color and design.

3. Look at all the beads made by the class and have the class describe each by its attributes.

4. Glue each bead onto a bigger sheet of paper.

5. Put the pages in order of a pattern, with each child's description of his or her pattern underneath.

Literature Extensions

String of Beads by Margarette S. Reid (Dutton, 1997)

Children in a Row

PURPOSE

To form and repeat a pattern.

MATERIALS

☆ 24" x 24" pocket chart

☆ 4 sentence strips (optional: 2 different colors)

☆ 20 children templates: 5 of each (pages 65–66)

☆ tagboard

☆ markers or crayons

☆ scissors

☆ glue

SETUP

1 Write words on sentence strips. If possible, use two different colors to emphasize the rhyme pattern.

2 Copy the children templates so that you have a minimum of 20 children. Color the children so that the stripes, spots, and plaid stand out. Glue the children onto tagboard. When the glue is dry, cut them out.

Pocket Chart Sentence Strips

Stripe, stripe, spot,

Plaid, line, dot.

Children in a row

Make the pattern grow.

by Valerie SchifferDanoff

3 Place words and 3–4 children in the chart, just enough to start the pattern of your choice.

LESSON

1 Discuss the word grow. Emphasize the different things that grow (children and plants, for example) and that when things grow, they increase in size.

2 Read the poem. Help children recognize what the word *grow* means in the poem.

3 Say the words in the poem that describe the attributes of the children's shirts: stripes, spots, and so on. Invite a child up to the chart to identify the cutout child whose shirt matches one of the attribute words. Repeat this until all of the attribute words have been linked to a cutout child.

4 While directing attention to the chart, ask, "How can we make this pattern grow?"

Hold up several different chart children and invite children from the class to choose which would come next. Then have children place the cutout in the chart. Continue until the chart is filled.

Hands-On and Follow-Up Activities

☆ Sort the children in class by clothing attributes such as colors, pants, T-shirts, and patterns. Make a real-life "Children in a Row" pattern.

☆ Make a new pattern using manipulative materials.

☆ Go on a pattern walk in the classroom or outside.

☆ Make a Pattern Big Book.

1. Ask children to dress in particular patterns for a day of more pattern activities.

2. Take photographs of the class during the day, and use them to make patterns in a class big book.

Literature Link

My Mom and Dad Make Me Laugh by Nick Sharratt (Candlewick, 1994)

Seashells, Seashells

PURPOSE

To represent patterns with numbers.

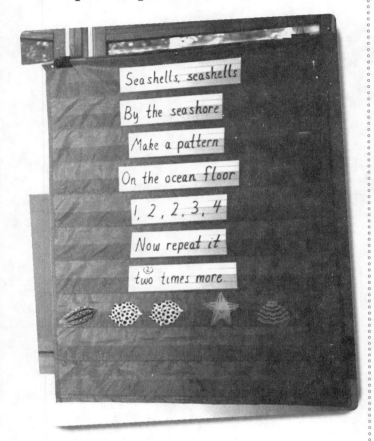

MATERIALS

☆ 24" x 24" pocket chart

☆ 5–7 sentence strips

☆ seashell templates: 5 copies of each (page 67)

☆ tagboard or construction paper

☆ scissors

☆ glue

☆ markers or crayons

Note: Real seashells are great, if available.

Pocket Chart Sentence Strips

Seashells, seashells,

By the seashore,

Make a pattern

On the ocean floor,

1, 2, 2, 3, 4.

Now repeat it

two times more.

by Valerie SchifferDanoff

SETUP

1 Write words on sentence strips.

2 Copy the seashell templates five times. Color the seashells and glue them onto tagboard. Make 20–30 seashells.

3 Place five shells in the chart in a 1, 2, 2, 3, 4 pattern; for example, star, conch, conch, clam, cone type.

LESSON

1 Say the poem. It's very catchy and may remind your class of the tongue twister "Sally sells seashells by the seashore." This could be used as a warm-up.

2 The numbers are the key element here in identifying and connecting the pattern to mathematical relationships. Invite children to make that connection with the seashells. Ask: "Which shells do we have only one of? Which shells do we have two of?"

3 Then work with the class and individual volunteers to extend the pattern on the chart.

Follow-Up Activities

☆ Transfer the number pattern to other manipulative materials, including the ones from the two previous charts.

☆ Reread the poem and substitute different numbers.

☆ Give each child a sentence strip with a number pattern on it. Have them make the pattern from manipulative materials.

☆ Copy seashells. Cut out and glue a pattern onto sentence strips. Do this as a whole-class activity. Then give each child a sentence strip with seashells on it. Have them write a corresponding number pattern.

☆ Copy seashells on different-colored paper. Make about 12 shells for each child in the class. Children can color, cut out, and glue their own seashell pattern.

Literature Extension

Out of the Ocean by Debra Frasier (Harcourt Brace, 1998)

Shells of the World by A. P. H. Oliver (The Hamlyn Publishing Group, 1989)

Bead Templates

Copy each bead 5 times.

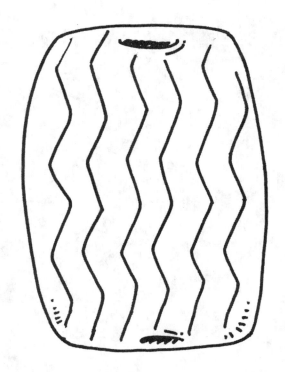

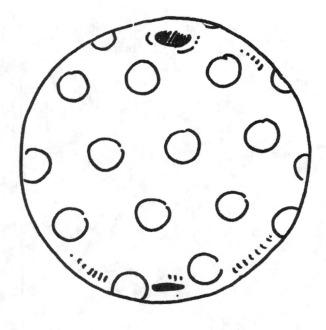

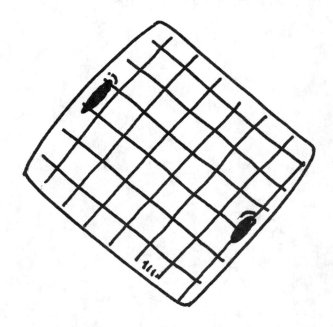

Children Templates

Copy each child 5 times.

Children Templates

Copy each child 5 times.

Pocket Charts for Math Scholastic Professional Books

Seashells Template

Copy each shell 5 times.

Notes

Notes

Notes